U.S. Department of Justice
Office of Justice Programs
810 Seventh Street NW.
Washington, DC 20531

Janet Reno
Attorney General

Daniel Marcus
Acting Associate Attorney General

Mary Lou Leary
Acting Assistant Attorney General

Nancy E. Gist
Director, Bureau of Justice Assistance

**Office of Justice Programs
World Wide Web Home Page**
www.ojp.usdoj.gov

**Bureau of Justice Assistance
World Wide Web Home Page**
www.ojp.usdoj.gov/BJA

For grant and funding information contact
U.S. Department of Justice Response Center
1–800–421–6770

This document was prepared by Community Research Associates, Inc., under grant number 95-DD-BX-K001, awarded by the Bureau of Justice Assistance, Office of Justice Programs, U.S. Department of Justice. The opinions, findings, and conclusions or recommendations expressed in this document are those of the authors and do not necessarily represent the official position or policies of the U.S. Department of Justice.

The Bureau of Justice Assistance is a component of the Office of Justice Programs, which also includes the Bureau of Justice Statistics, the National Institute of Justice, the Office of Juvenile Justice and Delinquency Prevention, and the Office for Victims of Crime.

INVESTING WISELY IN CRIME PREVENTION
INTERNATIONAL EXPERIENCES

September 2000

NCJ 182412

Prepared by Irvin Waller and Daniel Sansfaçon
International Centre for the Prevention of Crime

From the Director

At the end of a century that has seen unprecedented levels of crime, violence, and drug abuse in communities across America, we can take hope from the growing number of communities now reporting significant declines in their crime rates. We know that, at the community level, this success is due largely to crime reduction partnerships that contain strong prevention components. However, we still face many challenges to ridding our communities of crime.

First, the media's preoccupation with violent and frightening crimes leaves us all with a feeling of apprehension over the safety of our homes, workplaces, and schools. So although communities may be safer today than they were a few years ago, people still feel unsafe, and their perceptions, real or unreal, must be addressed. Second, despite the recent reductions in crime and violence, crime rates are still at unacceptably high levels, and we must not become complacent. Third, some communities have been left behind in this success—communities in which crime and violence are still on the rise.

We must find ways to meet these challenges head on by funding crime prevention programs that work. This monograph examines a variety of successful programs from around the world: the United Kingdom, France, the Netherlands, and New Zealand. These programs demonstrate that focused policing and mobilization of a broad range of agencies can significantly reduce crime rates. It is our hope that practitioners in the United States can learn from these experiences and develop crime reduction and prevention programs that are both financially and socially beneficial.

Nancy E. Gist
Director
Bureau of Justice Assistance

Acknowledgments

This monograph is based on a comparative analysis of successful crime prevention activities presented in *Crime Prevention Digest II*, prepared by the International Centre for the Prevention of Crime (ICPC) in Montreal, Canada. The analysis was made possible through the financial support of the National Crime Prevention Centre of Canada, as well as through core contributions to ICPC from the Home Office (England and Wales, United Kingdom), the Délégation Interministérielle à la Ville et au Développement Social Urbain (Interministerial Delegation for Social Development of Inner Cities) (France), Ministries of Justice and Interior and Kingdom Relations (the Netherlands), and the Ministry of Public Safety (Province of Quebec, Canada). Expert advice and comments were received from board members of ICPC, particularly those of the National Crime Prevention Council (United States), Crime Concern (England), the European Forum for Urban Safety (France), and the United Nations Office at Vienna (Austria).

The Bureau of Justice Assistance and ICPC would like to acknowledge the contributions of the following individuals who provided comments: Frantz Denat, Margaret Shaw, and Claude Vézina of ICPC and Brandon Welsh of the Department of Criminal Justice, University of Massachusetts at Lowell.

Contents

I. Introduction 1
    Should America Look at International Experience
    To Improve Safety? 1
    Crime Trends Better, But Still Worse Than They Were 1
    Efforts To Reduce Crime Show Results 2

II. Risk Factors. 5
    Risk Factors Are Well Established, But Overlooked 5
    Projects That Tackle Risk Factors Achieve Big Reductions 6
    Tackling Risk Factors Pays Off 7

III. Country Examples: Keys to Success 11
    U.K. Turns to Prevention To Spend Better, Not More 12
    France Pioneered Local Prevention Contracts,
    Now Creates Prevention Jobs 13
    The Netherlands Uses Learning-Based Strategies 14
    New Zealand Puts Prevention Where It Matters Most. 14

IV. Conclusion: Good Governance for Crime Prevention 15

V. Bibliography/References 17

VI. For More Information. 19

I. Introduction

Should America Look at International Experience To Improve Safety?

Many rigorous evaluations have shown that prevention projects in the United States have reduced crime across the nation over the past decade (Sherman et al., 1997). However, more is needed to decrease crime rates to the levels of the 1950s and 1960s. On average, American families spend more than $4,000 each year to participate in criminal justice systems, install private security measures, replace stolen property, or repair harm to victims. Can this money be used more wisely? Some European countries have started to invest in crime prevention, and the United States may be able to learn from these experiences.

By a three to one margin, Americans are ready either to pay more taxes or to forgo a tax cut to provide children access to early childhood development programs and quality afterschool activities, because they believe these programs greatly reduce violence (National Crime Prevention Council, 1999). Should public funds be invested in these programs to make America safer?

This monograph provides an analysis of opportunities for further reducing crime in the United States by looking at trends in the United Kingdom (U.K.), the Netherlands, France, and New Zealand. It focuses on the economic returns Americans may receive from investing in prevention.

The report is based on *Crime Prevention Digest II: Comparative Analysis of Successful Community Safety*, produced by the International Centre for the Prevention of Crime (ICPC) (Sansfaçon and Welsh, 1999). ICPC is an independent, nongovernmental organization supported by government agencies in Europe and North America. Representatives of the U.S. National Crime Prevention Council (NCPC) and the U.S. Conference of Mayors are members on its board of directors.

Crime Trends Better, But Still Worse Than They Were

Like other Western democracies in Europe, Australia, and Canada, the United States has seen a gradual decline in crime rates in the 1990s. Because of the rapid rise in crime rates in the 1960s and 1970s, however, today's rates are double or triple those of the early 1960s.

Members of households become the victims of such property crimes as burglaries or car thefts at similar rates on both sides of the Atlantic. The most recent comparative survey was taken in 1996 showing 1 residential burglary for every 38 adults in the United States and the Netherlands, 1 for every 42 adults in France, and 1 for every 33 adults in the U.K. (Mayhew and van Dijk, 1997).

Unfortunately, at 8 per 100,000 population the homicide rate in America is 4 times the rates of West European countries, which are between 1 and 2 per 100,000.

In the past four decades, the response to crime in the Western World has been primarily from law enforcement agencies and criminal justice systems. The Bureau of Justice Statistics (BJS) reports that "expenditures for each of the major criminal justice functions (police, corrections, judicial) has been increasing" steadily for several decades (Bureau of Justice Statistics, 2000).

In the United States and Western Europe, most offenders who are prosecuted and convicted for common offenses are disadvantaged men—typically in their late teenage or early adult years. Ultimately, many are incarcerated. The rate of adults in prisons and jails on an average day is one indicator of the use of incarceration as a sanction.

In 1970 the rate was 176 inmates per 100,000 population in the United States, compared with 80 in England, 59 in France, and 18 in the Netherlands. By 1998 these rates had grown to 645 in the United States, 125 in England, 90 in France, and 85 in the Netherlands—showing a significant increase in the gap between the United States and these European countries.

Efforts To Reduce Crime Show Results

From 1986 to 1996 property and violent crime rates in the United States decreased by a modest 7 percent. Yet in some U.S. cities, such as Fort Worth, New York, and Boston, they decreased dramatically—56 percent, 41 percent, and 29 percent, respectively.

Some argue that increases in employment rates, decreases in the proportion of Americans between the ages of 15 and 25 (an age group prone to crime), and the large numbers of persons incarcerated account for these reductions. They may in part, but cities like Fort Worth, New York, and Boston also implemented special initiatives to reduce crime, calling on their police departments to focus on crime reduction. They also have mobilized other agencies to work with disadvantaged youth and protect residences better against burglary and high-volume crime.

Cities in other countries, such as Canada and the U.K., also have seen such reductions. Again, these reductions appear to have been due to a combination of demographic trends, focused policing, and mobilization of a broad sector of agencies.

II. Risk Factors

Risk Factors Are Well Established, But Overlooked

Crime rates do not decrease simply by creating more jobs or improving policing services. Reducing crime requires a range of agencies to focus on multiple causes. Numerous studies in the United States, the U.K., and the Netherlands, as well as reports prepared by the United Nations, have concluded that several risk factors are associated with increases in crime.

For instance, large-scale longitudinal surveys on both sides of the Atlantic have studied how the development of individuals from birth to adulthood affects their propensity to be involved with crime. Studies have shown that a small group of individuals (5 to 10 percent) accounts for most offenses (50 to 70 percent) committed each year. Researchers have concluded that youth exposed to any or all of the following conditions are more likely to commit delinquent acts than those who are not:

- Relative poverty and inadequate housing.
- Inconsistent and insufficient parental or guardian guidance.
- Limited social and cognitive abilities.
- Exclusion from school.
- Family violence.
- Few opportunities for employment and economic exclusion.
- A culture of violence.

Biennially in the U.K. and annually in the United States, large-scale surveys of the adult population are taken to determine the number, location, and characteristics of victims of crimes. These surveys involve hundreds of thousands of persons.

The surveys show that a small proportion of neighborhoods account for a large number of crime incidents—in the U.K. 4 percent of neighborhoods account for 44 percent of incidents. Repeat victimization is common for victims of burglaries and car thefts, as well as domestic and street violence.

The surveys also show that victimization is not random. It happens more frequently under the following conditions:

- Residences and goods are inadequately protected.

- Goods are easy to transport and sell.
- Victim lives with the offender.
- Alcohol or substance abuse is involved.
- Firearms are available.

Finally, the surveys show that information about crime prevention is not used systemically. Fads and popular notions guide action more than facts.

Projects That Tackle Risk Factors Achieve Big Reductions

In England, the United States, and the Netherlands careful evaluations of some of these risk factors conclude that delinquency can be reduced effectively. Del Elliott's Blueprints Program at the University of Colorado at Boulder has identified 10 of the most effective early childhood and youth programs for reducing delinquency. These include the Midwestern Prevention Program, Big Brothers/Big Sisters, Functional Family Therapy, Quantum Opportunities, Life Skills Training, Multi-systemic Therapy, Nurse Home Visitation, Treatment Foster Care, Bullying Prevention Program, and PATHS (Promoting Alternative THinking Strategies) (University of Colorado, 2000).

When treating young children and their parents, the following interventions have proved useful:

- Using preschool and afterschool programs to increase the cognitive and social abilities of children, particularly in underprivileged social environments.
- Visiting at-risk families at home to improve parenting skills (particularly of young, single, low-income mothers with limited schooling).
- Increasing support and assistance for parents.

The following interventions are used with school-age children:

- Improving cognitive and social skills through at-home visits by teachers and structured recreational and cultural activities.
- Providing incentives to complete secondary studies by offering educational and financial assistance.
- Improving self-esteem and social integration capacity through neighborhood programs such as Big Brothers/Big Sisters and Boys & Girls Clubs.
- Offering on-the-job training and opportunities.
- Organizing school and after-school activities to decrease violent behavior.
- Working with families of first-time youthful offenders to decrease domestic dysfunction.

Several projects have demonstrated success at reducing common crimes, such as residential burglaries and car thefts. The following approaches have been effective at preventing residential burglary:

- "Cocoon" neighborhood watch.

- Improvements in home security and etching owners' names on household items.

- Treatment of substance-abusing offenders.

- Analysis of and intervention for repeat victims.

For public disorder and incivilities, a number of approaches have achieved reductions:

- Vandalism has been reduced through measures that hold youth accountable for their delinquent behavior.

- Cheating on public transportation has been reduced by increasing personnel and surveillance at transit stations.

- Incivilities have been reduced by placing closed-circuit cameras in problem areas.

- Fights and physical assaults have been reduced near bars by holding owners partially responsible and requiring them to take various measures.

Several measures have been introduced to help people, particularly women, feel safe in public places. Initial assessments reveal that the following measures show promise:

- Hiring more staff to provide information and surveillance in public areas in cities.

- Modifying public transportation routes.

- Improving lighting on streets.

Tackling Risk Factors Pays Off

In addition to being effective, the measures described above are usually more cost-effective than traditional crime control measures, such as incarceration. Economic evaluations of crime prevention programs show that:

- Actions encouraging the social development of children, youth, and families reduce delinquent behavior with returns ranging from $1.06 to $7.16 for every $1 spent (Sansfaçon and Welsh, 1999).

- Actions aiming to reduce opportunities for victimization have produced returns ranging from $1.83 to $7.14 for every $1 spent (Sansfaçon and Welsh, 1999).

As well as decreasing delinquency, reducing the number of offenses, and increasing social integration, these measures also generated economic benefits for various government sectors:

- More people were employed so more taxable income was generated.

- More housing was rented, increasing residency rates as well as economic investment in the community.

- Demand for criminal justice services decreased.

- Less social and health-care assistance was required.

In England, a survey by the Audit Commission (1996) on the cost-effectiveness of various measures to treat young persons showed that judicial intervention costs $10,542, compared with $6,950 for an enhanced school program (helping youth dropouts to return to the school) and $1,167 for programs to help youth find jobs.

In the United States, the RAND Corporation (Greenwood et al., 1996) analyzed the costs and benefits of five approaches to veering youth from a life of crime. ICPC was able to use the data to determine the tax increase per family that would be needed to reduce crime by 10 percent. The study found that $228 in extra taxes would be required for incarceration, $118 for probation, $48 for special parent training, and $32 for incentives to help at-risk youth complete school (figure 1).

Like countries in Western Europe, the United States spends more on education and health than on justice and crime, but because of the

Figure 1
Extra Taxes Needed for a 10-Percent Reduction in Crime

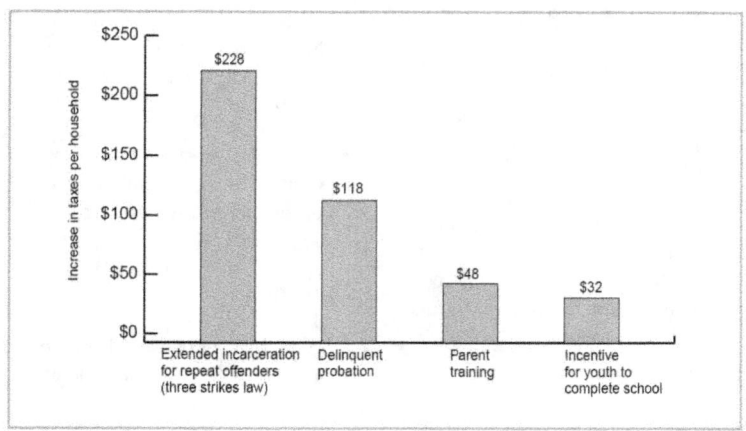

meteoric rise in incarceration in the United States, incarceration expenditures may soon exceed education expenditures. Another study by RAND shows that, at current rates of growth, expenditures on incarceration in California will rise from 9 percent of the state budget in 1994 to 17 percent in 2002, while the funds available for higher education will drop from 12 percent to 1 percent (Sansfaçon and Welsh, 1999).

In the Netherlands a simulation model comparing four scenarios to reduce crime by 10 percent showed that investing in prevention through social development was more effective than the addition of 1,000 police officers (van Dijk, 1997). On this basis, the Dutch government reallocated $100 million over 5 years to reinforce social prevention.

III. Country Examples: Keys to Success

Broad consensus exists in the international community on the process needed to ensure cost-effective action. The United Nations and international organizations comprising local elected officials, leaders of police organizations, judges, community groups, governmental experts, and service providers have identified the same set of procedures for successfully and effectively preventing crime.

At the heart of the process is a responsible central organization that brings together key departments (justice, education, health, social services, housing and urban planning, community organizations, and citizens). With strong leadership, this organization sets in motion a rigorous process of diagnosis, development of an action plan, implementation, and assessment and evaluation (figure 2).

This process rests on two fundamental elements. First, studies of risk factors and the actions that reduce them show that these factors are interrelated and that many sectors must agree on how to respond to them. Efforts should not concentrate on implementing a specific measure, but rather should set in motion a battery of interventions that will target the risk factors. For this reason, it is important to mobilize several partners.

Figure 2
Key Elements of Successful Crime Prevention

Second, analysis of successful action shows that such sectors as education, health, social services, entertainment, housing, transportation, justice, and police should initiate action in their respective areas in collaboration with other sectors.

The remainder of this chapter presents brief descriptions of how the U.K., France, the Netherlands, and New Zealand have used this process to prevent crime.

U.K. Turns to Prevention To Spend Better, Not More

In 1997 the British Treasury said "no more" to rising expenditures unless they would reduce crime. It undertook a comprehensive spending review using American, British, and Dutch evaluations and analysis by the International Centre for the Prevention of Crime. This review identified programs that had significantly reduced crime by investing in prevention. It showed evidence that particular preventive approaches were more cost-effective than paying for more intervention and detention (Goldblatt and Lewis, 1998).

Her Majesty's Inspectorate of Constabulary (1998)—comprising experienced police chiefs in the U.K.—examined the success of British police in reducing crime. Police forces that had achieved a 40-percent reduction in crime over 5 years without an increase in personnel had used problem-solving policing and partnerships with other organizations. Written under the chairmanship of John Stevens, head of Scotland Yard, the review found that significant policing was still reactive despite the interest in preventive tools.

A report by the Audit Commission (1996)—a governmental watchdog on local government spending—reported that funding for youth crime was being misspent. Funding was going to inefficient responses after the harm was done, rather than to programs that involved children in their early years when chances were good that they could be diverted from a life of crime. The Audit Commission agreed with research conducted for the U.S. Congress showing that the main impact of incarceration is to incapacitate offenders by placing them behind bars and that jail experience has little effect on reducing crime, as offenders relapse into crime at a high rate within the first 2 years of their release (Sherman et al., 1997).

As a result, the British Treasury allocated the equivalent of 5 percent of spending ($7 per household per year) on enforcement and deterrence to a new crime reduction program based on proven ways of reducing crime. Ten percent of this money was to be spent on evaluating the costs and benefits of the investment (Home Office, 1999). The program focuses on the following:

- Establishing programs for families, children, and schools to prevent youth from offending.

Country Examples: Keys to Success

- Tackling high-volume crime (e.g., burglary) in communities.
- Redesigning consumer products so that they are difficult to steal.
- Implementing more effective sentencing.

All city government officials and police managers were required to cooperate on a new community safety approach to reduce crime. This effort required city government and police services to collaborate on a safety diagnosis, the design and implementation of a community safety strategy, and the evaluation of the results. These tasks were coordinated with other social policies of the government. This national "crusade" was to be tough on crime and its causes.

France Pioneered Local Prevention Contracts, Now Creates Prevention Jobs

In 1983 the French government developed a national crime prevention policy. It set up a national crime prevention council to coordinate the crime prevention efforts of a broad range of ministries, such as law enforcement, justice, education, youth, and housing. This council had funds to form contracts with mayors to support local crime prevention projects that would develop a broad committee organization chaired by the mayor and that would analyze local problems to tackle situations that led to crime.

In the 1980s many local councils were developed.

In 1989 the functions of the national crime prevention council were integrated into a broader based policy on urban and social development, managed by the interministerial secretariat. Crime prevention became a component of policies on housing, health, education, culture, and recreation. The council continues to form contracts with mayors each year on a range of urban issues, including security and justice.

In 1997, the national cabinet committee on safety and security decided to reenergize the process and find a better balance between social prevention and community safety by proposing contracts to be signed by the mayor, the chief prosecutor, the police chief, and, in many cases, the national official for education.

Approximately 450 contracts have been signed, covering most urban areas in France. A total of 700 are expected. Many smaller communities have local crime prevention councils and are also expected to draw up contracts in the future. The contracts foster crime prevention through projects involving social integration, employment, and support for parents, as well as access to justice and victim assistance through community justice centers *(maison de justice)*. The national government has made funds available to local communities to employ 35,000 youth who work with police as safety and security assistants or as social mediation agents in communities.

The Netherlands Uses Learning-Based Strategies

The Netherlands has specialized in testing innovative crime prevention efforts in local projects. If evaluation results show that a particular effort works, the results are publicized and communities across the country are encouraged to try this activity. For instance, when results showed that setting particular design standards for houses reduced the number of houses burglarized in the early 1990s, the standards were promoted nationally.

Another example is a program called HALT. Through this program juveniles involved in vandalism are required by the police or the prosecuting authority to repair the damage and seek assistance. Evaluations show that the program reduces recidivism, and the program has been established in 65 sites.

The current policy to prevent youth violence has been influenced by results from the United States. It follows three tracks:

- A structured and inclusive national action directed at reducing delinquency among minority youth.

- A structured program of action to lower secondary school dropout rates and to facilitate employment of at-risk youth.

- A structured program to give children and teenagers a healthy start.

New Zealand Puts Prevention Where It Matters Most

In 1993 New Zealand created a crime prevention unit within the Prime Minister's office. The unit has an annual budget of more than $3 million to allow local communities to establish community safety partnerships, called Safer Community Councils. It also influences the allocation of government resources to prevent crime. The unit has assisted in developing more than 60 Safer Community Councils.

IV. Conclusion: Good Governance for Crime Prevention

For too long, we have left the problems of crime to law enforcement and criminal justice. However, research has shown that other sectors—such as schools, social services, entertainment, health services, and business—are also important partners in crime prevention efforts.

Good governance for crime prevention ensures that organizations are mobilized to take on the necessary responsibility. Whether at the city, state, or federal level, a central crime prevention organization is needed to be responsible for intersectoral work that brings together different agencies, stimulates partnerships, facilitates the dissemination of knowledge and tools, and encourages monitoring and reassessment.

The central crime prevention organization (figure 2) translates the initial messages from leaders into practical strategies for communities. Strategies should:

- Elaborate a plan of action with defined priorities and targets.

- Influence the policies and decisions of relevant organizations.

- Stimulate and sustain community partnerships.

To develop a practical strategy, the central crime prevention organization must have:

- The capacity to analyze trends in crime, identify risk factors and ways to address them effectively, and organize a rigorous assessment of the actions.

- Resources to invest in pilot projects, sustain action, disseminate information, and foster training.

- The ability to ensure coordination among the various sectors.

- The means to inform the public and change practices if necessary.

Some cities in the United States, like those in Europe, have achieved remarkable reductions in crime. Despite some decreases, crime levels remain unacceptable.

Many agreed that the causes of crime must be tackled. If demonstration projects tackle those causes, crime will decrease. In many cases, community demonstration projects are more cost-effective than existing law enforcement and incarceration measures. The demonstration projects, however, are often not sustained.

The benchmarks for successful crime prevention strategies have been well established by experts and intergovernmental commissions. Unfortunately, fads and conventional wisdom, rather than proven methods, dominate innovations for diagnosing the problem and mobilizing the agencies that can solve it.

Some countries have started national strategies to reduce crime through prevention. The latest hard-hitting program in the U.K. invests in prevention. The Netherlands invests in efforts that have proved successful. In France education, housing, and law enforcement agencies tackle the risk factors together.

The United States can benefit from experiences of practitioners not only in the United States but also in other countries committed to reducing crime through prevention.

V. Bibliography/References

Audit Commission. 1996. *Misspent Youth . . . Young People and Crime*. London, England: Audit Commission.

Bureau of Justice Statistics. 2000. "Summary Findings." *Expenditure and Employment Statistics*. Retrieved June 12, 2000. www.ojp.usdoj.gov/bjs/eande.htm.

Council of Europe. 1988. Final Declaration. Paper presented at the Conference on the Reduction of Urban Insecurity, November 17–20. Barcelona, Spain.

Crime Concern. 1993. *A Practical Guide to Crime Prevention for Local Partnerships*. London, England: Home Office.

European Forum for Urban Safety, Federation of Canadian Municipalities, and the United States Conference of Mayors. 1991. Final Declaration. Paper presented at the Second International Conference on Urban Safety, Drugs, and Crime Prevention, November 18–20. Paris, France.

European Forum for Urban Safety, Federation of Canadian Municipalities, and United States Conference of Mayors. 1989. Agenda for Safer Cities: Final Declaration. Paper presented at the European and North American Conference on Urban Safety, Drugs, and Crime Prevention, October 10–13. Montreal, Canada.

Gauthier, L.A., D. Hicks, D. Sansfaçon, and L. Salel. 1999. *100 Promising Crime Prevention Programs From Across the World*. Montreal, Canada: International Centre for the Prevention of Crime.

Goldblatt, P., and C. Lewis, eds. 1998. *Reducing Offending: An Assessment of Research Evidence on Ways of Dealing With Offending Behaviour*. London, England: Home Office, Research and Statistics Directorate.

Greenwood, P.W., K.E. Model, C.P. Rydell, and J. Chiesa. 1996. *Diverting Children From a Life of Crime: Measuring Costs and Benefits*. Santa Monica, CA: RAND Corporation.

Her Majesty's Inspectorate of Constabulary. 1998. *Beating Crime*. London, England: Home Office.

Home Office. 1999. *Crime Reduction Strategy*. London, England: Home Office.

Linden, Rick. 1996. *A Safer Canada: Guide for Community Crime Prevention*. Ottawa, Canada: National Crime Prevention Council of Canada.

Loeber, R., and D.P. Farrington. 1998. "Never Too Early, Never Too Late: Risk Factors and Successful Interventions for Serious and Violent Juvenile Offenders." *Studies on Crime and Crime Prevention* 7(1): 7–30.

Mayhew, P., and J.J.M. van Dijk. 1997. *Criminal Victimisation in Eleven Industrialised Countries*. The Hague, the Netherlands: Research and Documentation Centre, Ministry of Justice.

National Crime Prevention Council. 1999. *Saving Money While Stopping Crime*. Washington, DC: National Crime Prevention Council.

Newman, G., ed. 1999. *Global Report on Crime and Justice*. Oxford, England: Oxford University Press.

Reiss, A.J., and J.A. Roth, eds. 1993. *Understanding and Preventing Violence*. Washington, DC: National Academy Press.

Sansfaçon, D., and B. Welsh. 1999. *Crime Prevention Digest II: Comparative Analysis of Successful Community Safety*. Montreal, Canada: International Centre for the Prevention of Crime.

Sherman, L., D. Gottfredson, D. MacKenzie, J. Eck, P. Reuter, and S. Bushway. 1997. *Preventing Crime: What Works, What Doesn't, What's Promising*. Washington, DC: U.S. Department of Justice. NCJ 165366.

University of Colorado. 2000. "Ten Model Programs." *Blueprints for Violence Prevention*. Retrieved June 8, 2000. www.colorado.edu/cspv/blueprints/model/Default.htm.

van Dijk, J.J.M. 1997. "Towards a Research-Based Crime Reduction Policy: Crime Prevention as a Cost-Effective Policy Option." *European Journal on Criminal Policy and Research* 5(3): 13–27.

VI. For More Information

Please use the contact information below to learn more about the programs discussed in this monograph, as well as other national crime prevention programs.

Australia
Law Enforcement Group
Law Enforcement Coordination Division
Robert Garran Offices
National Circuit
Barton, Canberra 2600
Australia
61-2-6250-6772
Fax: 61-2-6273-0914
E-mail: cathy.rossiter@ag.gov.au

Belgium
Secrétariat Permanent à la Politique de Prévention
Ministère de l'Intèrieur
26, rue de la Loi
Brussels 1040
Belgium
32-2-500-24-41
Fax: 32-2-500-24-47
E-mail: info@belgium.fgov.be

Canada
National Crime Prevention Centre
Department of Justice of Canada
275 Sparks Street, Fifth Floor
Ottawa, Ontario K1A 0H8
Canada
613-957-9639
Fax: 613-952-3515
E-mail: Mary-Anne.kirvan@ justice.gc.ca

England and Wales
Policing and Reducing Crime Unit
Home Office
Clive House, Room 419
Petty France
London SW1H 9HD
England
44-207-271-8901
Fax: 44-207-271-8344
E-mail: CaroleF.Willis@homeoffice. gsi.gov.uk

France
Délégation Interministérielle à la Ville et au Développement Social Urbain
194, Avenue du President Wilson
St-Denis-La Plaine 93217
France
33-1-49-17-46-10
Fax: 33-1-49-17-46-90
E-mail: didier.michal@ville.gouv.fr

Ivory Coast
Conseil National de Sécurité
01 B.P. 518
Abidjan
Ivory Coast
225-32-24-77/78
Fax: 225-32-12-24
E-mail: gtanny@globeaccess.net

The Netherlands
Policy Department
Ministry of Justice
P.O. Box 20301
The Hague 2515 EX
The Netherlands
31-70-370-79-11
Fax: 31-70-370-79-75
E-mail: wmeurs@best-dep.minjust.nl

Department of Public Safety,
  Information Policy & Projects
Ministry of the Interior & Kingdom
  Relations
P.O. Box 20011
The Hague 2500 EA
The Netherlands
31-70-426-68-17
Fax: 426-61-62
E-mail: Derk.Oosterzee@minbiza.nl

Portugal
Gabinete de Assuntos Europeus
Ministerio da Administraçao Interna
Praça do Comercio
Lisbon 1149-015
Portugal
351-1-32-32-062
Fax: 351-1-343-15-96
E-mail: gae@meganet.pt

South Africa
Secretariat for Safety and Security
P.O. Box 413460
Craighall
Johannesburg, South Africa
27-11-325-4556
Fax: 11-325-4607
E-mail: bfanaroff@resolve.co.za

International Center for the Prevention of Crime
507, Place d'Armes, Suite 2100
Montreal, Quebec
Canada H2Y 2W8
514-288-6731
Fax: 514-288-8763
E-mail: cipc@crime-prevention-
  intl.org

National Crime Prevention Council
1000 Connecticut Avenue NW.
13th Floor
Washington, DC 20036
202-466-6272
Fax: 202-296-1356
World Wide Web: www.ncpc.org

For additional information on BJA grants and programs contact:

Bureau of Justice Assistance
810 Seventh Street NW.,
  Fourth Floor
Washington, DC 20531
202-514-6278
Fax: 202-305-1367
World Wide Web:
www.ojp.usdoj.gov/BJA

Bureau of Justice Assistance Clearinghouse
P.O. Box 6000
Rockville, MD 20849-6000
1-800-688-4252
World Wide Web: www.ncjrs.org

Clearinghouse staff are available Monday through Friday, 8:30 a.m. to 7 p.m. eastern time. Ask to be placed on the BJA mailing list.

U.S. Department of Justice Response Center
1-800-421-6770 or 202-307-1480

Response Center staff are available Monday through Friday, 9 a.m. to 5 p.m. eastern time.

Bureau of Justice Assistance Information

General Information

Callers may contact the U.S. Department of Justice Response Center for general information or specific needs, such as assistance in submitting grant applications and information on training. To contact the Response Center, call 1–800–421–6770 or write to 1100 Vermont Avenue NW., Washington, DC 20005.

Indepth Information

For more indepth information about BJA, its programs, and its funding opportunities, requesters can call the BJA Clearinghouse. The BJA Clearinghouse, a component of the National Criminal Justice Reference Service (NCJRS), shares BJA program information with state and local agencies and community groups across the country. Information specialists are available to provide reference and referral services, publication distribution, participation and support for conferences, and other networking and outreach activities. The Clearinghouse can be reached by

- ❐ **Mail**
  P.O. Box 6000
  Rockville, MD 20849–6000

- ❐ **Visit**
  2277 Research Boulevard
  Rockville, MD 20850

- ❐ **Telephone**
  1–800–688–4252
  Monday through Friday
  8:30 a.m. to 7 p.m.
  eastern time

- ❐ **Fax**
  301–519–5212

- ❐ **Fax on Demand**
  1–800–688–4252

- ❐ **BJA Home Page**
  www.ojp.usdoj.gov/BJA

- ❐ **NCJRS World Wide Web**
  www.ncjrs.org

- ❐ **E-mail**
  askncjrs@ncjrs.org

- ❐ **JUSTINFO Newsletter**
  E-mail to listproc@ncjrs.org
  Leave the subject line blank
  In the body of the message, type:
  subscribe justinfo
  [your name]

www.ingramcontent.com/pod-product-compliance
Lightning Source LLC
Chambersburg PA
CBHW071016200526
45171CB00007B/293